LIFE'S A DREAM

by
CALDERÓN

Adapted
by
ADRIAN MITCHELL
and
JOHN BARTON

Dramatic Publishing
Woodstock, Illinois • London, England • Melbourne, Australia

INTRODUCTION

Calderón de la Barca
or How I learned to stop worrying and love the Spanish Golden Age.

This introduction is not for scholars. They know far more
about Calderón than I do. It is for those people who find
themselves intimidated by the strangeness of Spain, even con-
temporary Spain, let alone the 17th Century Spain.

I felt that same nervousness only a few years ago. When I
first read about the plays of the Spanish Golden Age—from
around 1500 to 1681, the period in which Calderón, Lope de
Vega, Cervantes, Tirso de Molina and Rojas Zorilla flour-
ished—I was dumbfounded by the system of values, espe-
cially the "Honour" system which seemed to dominate the
drama. It was only when I began to read the plays thoroughly
that I discovered that you have to know very little about such
matters to understand many of the greatest plays. Honour is
such a strange word in England these days. Good name and
reputation are still far easier to handle.

But when you read or act or watch *The Mayor of Zalamea*
you need to know about human beings, not about social
codes. Of course, the more you know about the social back-
ground the more you'll understand and enjoy. But most of us
live in a world which doesn't allow time for historical re-
search in between work or looking for work and going to the
theatre. *The Mayor of Zalamea* was the first Spanish play I
attempted, using a literal translation by Gwenda Pandolfi,
sticking very closely to the text, using a kind of syllabic
verse. This was commissioned by the National Theatre. When
I read the play for the second time I knew that given a half-
decent production, it must be popular. Michael Bogdanov's
production was spare and strong and had at its centre a perfor-

mance of pure gold by Michael Bryant. The production proved that there is no difficulty for an English audience with at least one of the Golden Age plays. It started at the Cottesloe and transferred to the Olivier because more seats were needed.

After its success the National suggested another Calderón, *Life's a Dream*. But just as I was completing my version it was discovered that the Royal Shakespeare Company was about to stage a version of the same play by John Barton. I rang John, whom I didn't know at the time, to confirm that this was true, since the National had decided to scrap its plans. He is the most generous of bears and said something like: "Come on over and I'll show you mine and you show me yours." We both liked each other's versions. He'd solved problems I had been stumped by. I'd laid down some mean verse. John suggested mixing the versions together and that's what we did. He kept a kind of record of whose line was whose and it worked out about forty-six per cent John, forty-six percent Adrian and eight per cent lines which were a mixture of the two. His production was highly acclaimed both in Stratford and London and once again the availability of Spanish drama to an English audience was proved.

The Great Theatre of the World was commissioned by the Mediaeval Players. The metaphor of the play, in which God is a theatre director and the World is his stage manager appealed to me strongly. So did the humour and the pathos and the poetic wonder of the play—it is a Christian play but a pretty undogmatic one, naturally, since Calderón could take it for granted that he had a Christian audience.

The theatre is a real world. This has advantages and disadvantages. One given factor for this production was that the Players have developed many circus skills like juggling and stilt-walking. We used this by giving the play an interlude half way through in which, since the play is much possessed by death, skeletons danced and played, giant skeletons walked on bone-like stilts and juggler skeletons demonstrated their art with skulls and bones. Disadvantages—the Players' grant couldn't stretch to a complete cast. One character, I was told, had to be left out. I chose the one which I felt was least relevant to a modern audience, the character Discretion, who chooses a contemplative life. Don't blame me, blame Mrs. Thatcher. I suppose I could have written back Discretion into the play for this published edition. I decided not to. This is a version for Philistine Britain where even a very funny and affecting play about eternal truths has to lose, if not a limb, then a few fingers in the cause of cost-effectiveness.

Calderón lived from 1600 to 1681. To find out about his life and work, read his entry in the "Oxford Companion to Spanish Literature" and Gerald Brenan's wonderful "The Literature of the Spanish People."

His work is sometimes characterised as formal, intellectual, spiritual, maybe somewhat cold. All these things are true, but there is far more to his plays. They're certainly not cold, they simply seem comparatively cool when you place them beside the red hot passion of Lope de Vega. But there is a slow-burning passion in Calderón and also a lovely humour which is often forgotten. Lope de Vega (1562-1635) was surely a mixture of earth and fire. Calderón is air and water, a most beautiful fountain. And often, a fiery fountain.

ADRIAN MITCHELL

This collection is dedicated to all the theatre people involved in the first productions of these versions, with many thanks and much admiration.

This version of *Life's a Dream* was first performed at The Other Place, Stratford-upon-Avon on 23 November 1983 with the following cast:

Rosaura	Barbara Kellermann
Clarion	Anthony O'Donnell
Sigismund	Miles Anderson
Clotaldo	David Waller
Astolfo	Christopher Neame
Estrella	Lesley Duff
Basilio	Charles Kay
Soldiers, Courtiers, Servants	Jeremy Wilkin
	Richard Garnett
	David Killick
	Cyril Nri
Musicians	Michael Tubbs
	Bryan Allen
	Peter Hopkins
	Clifford Pick
Director	John Barton
Designer	Christopher Morley
Lighting	Leo Leibovici
Music	Guy Woolfenden
Voice work	Cicely Berry
	David Carey
Music Director	Michael Tubbs
Design Assistant	Jill Jowett
Stage Manager	Titus Grant
Deputy Stage Manager	Helen Lovat-Fraser
Assistant Stage Manager	Peter Miller

Based on literal versions by
Lucy Woolley and Gwenda Pandolfi.

LIFE'S A DREAM

A Play in Three Acts
For Five Men and Two Women, Extras

CHARACTERS

ROSAURA .... a confused woman
CLARION .... a foolish servant
SIGISMUND .... Prince of Poland
CLOTALDO .... his keeper
ASTOLFO .... Duke of Muscovy
ESTRELLA .... Princess of Poland
BASILIO .... King of Poland
SOLDIERS
COURTIERS
SERVANTS

ACT ONE

SCENE ONE

(A stage. Enter ROSAURA dressed as a man. She mounts a hobby horse and rides gently. Drums and trumpets sound suddenly and the horse neighs and goes wild. She tries to control it but it careers round the stage. She falls off.)

ROSAURA.   You're not a horse,
                    You're a hippogriff.
                    Why have you thrown me?
                    Coward, you shied and bucked
                    At a shadow, a nothing.
                    Flash without flame!
                    Fish without scales!
                    Bird without feathers!
                    You threw me on these rocks.
                    Stay in the mountains then:
                    Make friends with the wolves.
                    But what about me?
                    I'm lost…
                    Somewhere in Poland.
                    Somewhere in the mountains.
                    I'm a stranger.
                    I am tired from riding,
                    The sun is going down
                    And I've nobody for company
                    But Clarion the Clown.

(Enter CLARION.)

CLARION.　　　So this is Poland. What a place.
　　　　　　　About as friendly as outer space.
　　　　　　　Up there black crags, down there a gloomy
　　　　　　　　　lake.
　　　　　　　I'm hungry and thirsty and my shoulders
　　　　　　　　　ache.

ROSAURA.　　Trouble breeds trouble. We must endure it.

CLARION.　　　A hogshead of wine is the best way to cure it.
　　　　　　　Why did we leave our Muscovite nest
　　　　　　　To trudge round Europe on some crazy quest?

ROSAURA.　　You know very well
　　　　　　　Why we've come to Poland:
　　　　　　　To find my lost father
　　　　　　　And win back my honour.

CLARION *(sings).*
　　　　　　　I never had a father
　　　　　　　But if I had have done
　　　　　　　I'm sure he would have told me:
　　　　　　　"Be a man of honour, son."

　　　　　　　So I rose up one morning
　　　　　　　And hurried to the fair,
　　　　　　　For I had heard the rumour
　　　　　　　That the folk sold honour there.

　　　　　　　As I walked through the fairground
　　　　　　　My heart was struck by fear.

I heard a giant shouting
"Come and buy your honour here."

I asked him for some honour.
He laughed and turned away,
Said: "Honour is expensive
Son, are you prepared to pay?

"You pay your legs, your eyesight,
Your land, your house, your wife,
Your sanity, your children
And your money and your life."

I told him: "Keep your honour:
I don't want to be dead."
So I went and found a tavern
And I bought some wine instead.

ROSAURA.   Clarion, look there;
Look…do you see?
A tower hewn out of massive blocks
Lies at the centre of a maze of rocks
Like a chunk hewn out of solid midnight,
Or a great mill for grinding sunlight:
A tower darker than darkness.
(Sound of chains.)

CLARION.   Rosaura. Listen. Clanking.

ROSAURA.   I can't move. I'm freezing.
I can't move. I'm burning.

SIGISMUND (*cries out within*).
>I am unhappy.

CLARION.   Let us leave this tower.

ROSAURA.   Look. A flickering. A gleam
>In the blackness. Shifting, shimmering.
>There's a man, a wild man,
>In a tomb there or a dungeon.
>Let's hear what he has to say.

(*SIGISMUND comes forward, chained. He is carrying a picture-book.*)

SIGISMUND.   What have I done that I should suffer so?
>What crime have I committed? Tell me, stars.
>I have been born. Is that a crime in men?
>Were other men not born as I was born?
>Yet they are blessed and I have here no
>   blessings.
>(*Turns over the pages of the book.*)
>A bird is born, a swallow,
>Little and damp and shaken,
>It grows so bright and dark and feathery,
>A spray of flowers on the wing.
>It slices through the air so speedily
>That it outflies imagining
>And leaves its nest forsaken.
>Then why can't I
>Be like a swallow flying free?
>(*He turns the page to a picture of a salmon.*)
>A fish is born, a salmon.
>Child of the waterfall's rock and sprays.

Its rainbow armour fitting perfectly,
It cuts the oceans like a knife,
Charting and measuring the sea
And all the million forms of life
In the vast cold waterways.
Then why can't I
Be like a salmon swimming free?
(He turns the page to a picture of a waterfall.)
A spring is born, a stream,
Welling up among grass to go
As serpents travel, swift and windingly.
The river sings its silver thanks
And joys in its mobility
To flowers and beasts along its banks
As they watch its dazzling flow.
Then why can't I
Be like a river, flowing free?
(He turns to a picture of a leopard.)
A beast is born, a leopard,
Delicate as a hyacinth.
Its shaven hide is dappled cunningly
With paintbrush marks of black and gold.
But the grown leopard shows a cruelty
That's natural, so we are told,
A monster in a labyrinth.
Then why, why, can't I
Be like a leopard running free?

Born out of rage,
Eaten with rage,
I'm a volcano. Watch me bleed.
Give me a knife—I'll show you surgery
And wrench out, raggedy and raw

Bits of my heart. Captivity!
So is there some reason or some law
Denies me the one thing I need,
Which God gave swallows and salmon too,
And beasts and leopards: to be free?

ROSAURA.   What a sad story.

SIGISMUND.   Who's that? I can't see.
Clotaldo, is it you?

CLARION.   Go on, say it is,
But don't mention me.

ROSAURA.   We are travellers
Lost in this ravine
We heard your sorrow.

SIGISMUND.   So you know I'm weak?
Then you must die.

CLARION.   Would you repeat that? I didn't quite hear.
I'm a little bit deaf in my right ear.

SIGISMUND.   I'll tear you both in pieces.

ROSAURA.   I kneel. If you are human
I know that you will spare us.
We are humble creatures.

SIGISMUND.   Your voice is gentle. When I look on you
I find that I grow soft. You trouble me.
Who are you? O I know the world so little,

For I have spent my whole life in this prison,
If how I am is living. Since my birth
I have known nothing but this wilderness
Where I have lived alone, a living dead thing.
Till now I never spoke to anyone
But one old man who listens to my sorrows
And teaches me rare words and how to
    name things,
And tells me tales about the earth and sky.
But till today no one has calmed my anger,
O you have eased my eyes and charmed my
    ears,
For you refresh me and you make me wonder.

ROSAURA.   I do not know how I should answer you.
I'm full of wonder too…
What shall I say? Did Heaven lead me here
To see someone unhappier than myself?
I cannot tell and yet I think it must be.
There was a wise man once who lived on
    herbs:
"Can there be anyone," he asked himself,
"More poor and sad than I?" And then he saw
Another wise man picking up the leaves
That he had thrown away. He found his
    answer.
And so have I, for I have been complaining
Of this bad world, and you have answered me.
For what I think of as unhappiness
You would call joy, as if you picked my
    leaves up.
Then if you can find comfort from my sorrows
Take them and let me tell you who I am.

(Enter CLOTALDO. He fires a shot.)

CLOTALDO.   Guards! Soporific cowards!
     There are intruders in the tower.

CLARION.   More trouble.

SIGISMUND.   That's Clotaldo. He's my jailer.

CLOTALDO.   Place them under strict arrest
     And cut them down if they resist.

(Enter GUARDS with masked faces.)

CLARION.   I'm a completely lovable clown.
     I'll be very cut up if you cut me down.

CLOTALDO.   The King of Poland has decreed
     This a forbidden place
     And that the penalty is death
     To see this monster's face.
     Surrender to the guard
     Of the tower by the lake
     Or my pistol will tear out your throats
     Like a sudden snake.

SIGISMUND.   Do not harm them, master.
     You'll all die if you do,
     For with my nails and teeth
     I will fight with you.

CLOTALDO.   Sigismund, remember your own fate
     When you threaten homicide,

Heaven has decreed
When you were born, you died.
Remember this prison
Is a curb upon your pride.
Lock the tower door
And take him back inside.

SIGISMUND. Yes, heavens, you are right to steal my
                    freedom.
            If I was free I'd rise up like a giant
            And pile up stones and make a staircase
                    mountain
            And batter down the windows of the sun.

CLOTALDO. Perhaps your present sufferings are meant
            To stop you doing just that. Away with him.
            (GUARDS take SIGISMUND out.)
            Surrender to the guards.

ROSAURA. Here is my sword.
            I surrender it to you.
            I will not yield it
            Into less noble hands.

CLOTALDO. *My* sword's a bit bent
            And blunt at the end.
            It's a prize for a booby:
            Here you are, friend.
            *(CLARION gives the sword to a GUARD.
            CLOTALDO takes ROSAURA's. GUARD
            takes CLARION out.)*

ROSAURA. If I must die, sir,

Please guard it well.
It holds some great secret:
It is a legacy
From my lost father.

CLOTALDO.   And who was he?

ROSAURA.   I never knew him,
But I trust his sword,
And so I came to Poland,
For revenge on a man
Who has wronged my honour.

CLOTALDO *(takes his mask off. Aside).*
What is this, heavens?
I am flabbergasted.
All my own confusions,
My shame and my sorrows
Swamp my heart and mind.
Who gave it to you?

ROSAURA.   My mother.

CLOTALDO.   Her name?

ROSAURA.   I cannot tell you that.

CLOTALDO *(aside).*
Heaven help me! Can this be
Illusion or reality?
This is the sword I gave to my sweet love
When I was living still in Muscovy.
I swore that whosoever wore that sword

Would find me kind as if he was my son.
I am bewildered. Stranger, do not think
You are alone in your misfortunes here.
You must go in but I will use you gently.
(Exit ROSAURA.)
He has her eyes, as hot as shooting stars.
Now am I like a man locked in a room
Who hears a sound in the street and runs to
      the window.
My heart flies out of my eyes to stare at him.
I'm weeping. He's my son. What shall I do?
Let's work it out. One, he has offered me
My own good sword to win favour. Two,
By coming here he's brought his death day
      with him.
What must I do? O heavens, what must I do?
Take him before the King? That's certain
      death.
Hide him? I cannot, I should break my oath.
Now is it with me as in some old tale:
On one side, love, on one side, loyalty.
I'm torn. But why? I should not hesitate.
For loyalty to Kings is more than life
And more than honour. I believe that's true,
So do not mock me. What was it he said?
He came here to avenge some injury.
To leave an insult unavenged is shameful.
That is our code. Honour's so delicate,
A little breath, a puff of wind can smear it.
He is my son, my blood is in his veins:
What shall I do? I'll seek some middle way.
In this bad world that's best. I'll tell the King
This boy is mine. My loyalty may move him.

Then I can help him to avenge his honour.
But if the King is cruel, my son must die.
What's the worst fate the gods can give?
Some say to die, but others say…to live.

SCENE TWO

(Dawn. Drums and trumpets. Enter on one side ASTOLFO, Duke of Muscovy, attended, and on the other side PRIN-CESS ESTRELLA, also attended.)

ASTOLFO.   Estrella! Star-girl! Princess! Empress! Queen!
Your eyes are bright as comets. Drums and
    trumpets
Greet you and mix their homage with sweet
    nature.
Look how the birds and fountains blend
    their music
And all things wonder that behold your face.
Trumpets made of feathers, birds of brass
And the rough cannons hail you as their queen.
The birds cry out, "Look, that is bright
    Aurora,"
The trumpets, that Athene's here, the flowers
That you are Flora. O you mock the day
Even as the bright day mocks the banished
    night.
You are the dawn, Aurora, as you shine,
Athene as you war, in peace sweet Flora,
And all in all you are my proud heart's queen.

ESTRELLA. If deeds prove words, you will be proved a liar.
You do me wrong to flatter me, Astolfo.
Your courteous, amorous vocabulary
And your display of military might do not
    quite blend.
Your silver tongue talks love
But in your mind you dream of iron power.

ASTOLFO. No, you are wrong to doubt my faith, Estrella.
Fair cousin, hear me out. Basilio
Is King of Poland and a widower.
He is old now (Time mocks us all with age)
And more inclined to study than to women.
He has no child, so we both claim the throne...

ESTRELLA. I am the daughter of his eldest sister.

ASTOLFO. It's true I am the youngest sister's son,
For I was born to her in Muscovy,
Yet, being a man, I must take precedence.
This has been argued with our uncle King
Who says he means to reconcile us both,
And he has fixed this day and place to do it.
And that is why I've come from Muscovy.
Not to make war, though you make war on me
With all the weapons of your loveliness,
But to make love and win you, my Estrella.
If we two marry, Poland will be strong.

ESTRELLA. My heart thanks yours for your kind courtesy.
Yet I am only partly satisfied:
There is a picture hanging round your neck
Which rather gives the lie to what you say.

Do not confuse your longings for the throne
With other nicer longings of your own.

ASTOLFO.   I'll satisfy you fully as to that...
                  (Drums and trumpets sound.)
                  But may not do so now. The King is coming.

(Enter KING BASILIO, attended.)

                  O most wise King...

ESTRELLA.   O learned King...

ASTOLFO.   Who rules
                  Among the stars...

ESTRELLA.   The galaxies...

ASTOLFO.   The heavens...

ESTRELLA.   You plot the star-paths...

ASTOLFO.   Trace their fiery footsteps.

ESTRELLA.   You hear their music...

ASTOLFO.   And you read their meaning...

ESTRELLA.   O let me kneel before your royal feet.

ASTOLFO.   O let me press my lips upon your hand.

BASILIO.   Dutiful nephew, loving niece, embrace me.

You come in love and hope. However high
Your wishes soar you shall be satisfied.
So clear your minds of that, and all be silent.
Brave peers of Poland, vassals, kinsmen,
    friends.
You know already that for my deep wisdom
I am surnamed the Learned by the world,
And in defiance of Time's dusty heel
Painters and sculptors all around the globe
Create star-glowing images of me,
Which will outlive by tens of centuries
This fading face, these failing bones, this
    flesh:
Basilio the Learned. And the Great.
You know the science that I love the most:
The mathematics, by the means of which
I make a fool of Fate and cheat old Time,
Whose function is to unfold Fate itself.
I am the canny duellist who so far
Has always made the winning thrust. Poor
    Time,
His every stroke and counter-stroke is marked
Upon my charts ahead of him. I read him.
There are star mountains and I climb their
    peaks.
There are star forests and I know their paths,
And there are swamps and whirlpools made
    of stars.
Circles of snow, bright canopies of glass,
Cut by the moon, illumined by the sun,
These crystalline, concentric necklaces
These specks, these beads, these spirals,
    whirling tear-drops:

These are my life, my study and my passion,
These are my books, their diamond lettering
Printed upon bright sapphire-paper pages
By the great golden printing-press of Heaven.
I turn one blue page of the Universe
And, cruel or kind, there is our human future,
Easy to read as a child's alphabet.
And yet I wish, before I'd understood
The universe's simplest syllable,
The stars had poured their poison-fire on me.
A learned man's the victim of his learning.
For he who has foreknowledge of his fate
Murders himself and plays the suicide
In his own story. So perhaps with me.
Be silent still and hear me out with wonder.

I'm old now, but when I was young and fresh
I had a secret and unhappy son
At whose sad birth there was high rage in
    heaven.
Before the warm grave of his mother's womb
Transmitted him into the yellow daylight
(For birth and death are very much alike)
His mother dreamed a child monstrosity
Smeared with her life's blood, burst out of
    her entrails,
Took life and was her death. And when the day
Came for his birth, this omen was proved true:
In my experience, omens always are.
The sun was red as blood and fought the moon.
They took our planet as their wrestling-ground;
Silver and gold grappled and interlocked.
It was the greatest and most terrible

Of all the eclipses that the sun has suffered
Since it wept blood, mourning the death of
   Christ.
There was no star-fire in the firmament.
Palaces shook. And Sigismund was born.
He tore his mother's life out and so showed
His nature to the world as if to say,
"I repay good with evil. I'm a man."

I knew then he would grow up to be vicious.
A cruel prince and a despotic King;
That Poland would be torn by civil war
And that his wildness would debauch the
   Kingdom
Into a foul academy of chaos.
I knew he'd strike me down and use my beard
As if it were a carpet for his boots.
Who'd not believe such omens? I decided
That I must cage the beast and find out
   whether
One cunning King could overcome the stars.
I gave out that my son had died at birth.
I built a tower among night-black boulders
In a ravine beyond the reach of daylight,
And that is where he lives. The penalty
For trespassers is death without a trial.
He sees and talks with no one but Clotaldo
Who tutors him in science and religion
And is the only witness of his woes.

Three things must now be thought on. Pray
   you, mark me.

One, I love Poland and I won't allow her to
     be oppressed or crushed by tyranny.
Two, Christian charity: what right have I
To keep my son from that prerogative
Which by divine and human law is his?
Shall I turn criminal because of crimes
Which he has not committed, though he may?
Three, what if I have been too credulous?
What if he's gentle? The most cruel star
Can influence the will but cannot force it
Because a man's will is a gift from God.

I've wavered and I've weighed this, and I have
Devised a remedy which will amaze you.
I mean to set my son upon my throne
And to invest him with my royal power,
And you must all obey him as your King.
This stratagem can lead us to three outcomes
Which complement the three points I have
     made.
One, if he's prudent, wise and kind and gentle
And gives the lie to what is prophesied,
Then you shall have him as your own true
     King.
Two, if he proves reckless and cruel and wild
My moral obligation's at an end,
And it will seem in me a kind of mercy
To reimprison him, not punishment
But justice. Three, if that should be the
     outcome
I will ensure the Polish throne shall be
By you two occupied illustriously.
This, as I am your King, I now command

And, as I am his father, I require
And, as I am a wise man, I advise it,
And, as I'm old, I tell you blunt and plain.
And last, if Kings be slaves to their own
    kingdoms,
I, as your humble slave, beseech you all.

ASTOLFO.   Justice herself could form no plan more fair.

ESTRELLA.   God save the Prince and let him be your heir.

ASTOLFO.   Long live Basilio.

ESTRELLA.   God save the King.

ALL.   Long live Basilio. God save the King.
     (Music. Exit all but BASILIO.)

BASILIO.   I thank you for listening.
     We shall learn tomorrow
     Whether my son shall be a King
     Or whether he'll bring sorrow.

(Enter CLOTALDO with ROSAURA and CLARION chained and blindfolded.)

CLOTALDO.   A word, sire.

BASILIO.   Clotaldo. You are always welcome.
     What's wrong?

CLOTALDO.   My lord, a grievous thing has happened,
     Though in a sense it is a joyful thing...

BASILIO.   Go on.

CLOTALDO.   These two young men have seen the Prince.
                      They got into the tower...

BASILIO.   Don't fret, Clotaldo.
                      Since I have publicly proclaimed the truth,
                      Discovering the secret is no crime.
                      Attend me in an hour. I've much to tell you,
                      And you will have a busy day tomorrow,
                      For you must help me with the strangest act
                      The planet earth has seen. As for your
                          prisoners,
                      I will forgive you for your negligence.
                      Unbind their arms and eyes. You are all
                      pardoned.
                      (Exit.)

CLOTALDO.   God save the King
                      And may he live forever! Heaven is kind.
                      I thought it would be hard but it was easy.
                      (Aside.) I will not tell him that he is my son.
                      I did his mother wrong, and if he knew me
                      I fear he'd hate me. Strangers, you are free.

ROSAURA.   I kiss your feet, Your Grace.

CLARION.   I'll kiss you any place.

ROSAURA.   You saved my life.

CLARION.   I'll be your slave forever.

CLOTALDO.   Get up, both of you.
              (To CLARION.) Don't try to be clever.

CLARION.   I'm trying to be foolish.

CLOTALDO.   You've succeeded.

CLARION.   Why, then I'll be outside if I am needed.

CLOTALDO.   If needed I'll give you a clarion call.

CLARION.   Sir, you could be the biggest fool of them all.
              (Exit CLARION.)

ROSAURA.   You saved my life...

CLOTALDO.   You have no life. You say you have been
                 wronged,
              But noble men have neither life nor honour
              Until they are avenged. *(Aside.)* I see that I
              Must educate the boy. Sure, this will move
                 him.

ROSAURA.   I am not ashamed. I have done nothing wrong.

CLOTALDO.   Honour's not what you do
              But what is done to you.
              You can wash your face
              If it's splashed with mud
              But honour can only
              Be washed with blood.
              A man without honour's a mongrel pup

Snapping at fleas. *(Aside.)* That should stir
him up.

ROSAURA.   I will avenge my honour
And so win life.

CLOTALDO.   Well said.
Take back your sword.
Vow vengeance on your enemy.
That sword was mine
(I mean it was, just now)
It will serve you well:
Use it like a man.

ROSAURA.   Then in your name
I gird it on again
And swear as I am man
To be revenged on him
Who has wronged my honour.

CLOTALDO.   And I will likewise swear on oath to help you.

ROSAURA.   You would not say so if you knew his name.

CLOTALDO.   Have I not sworn it? Is it some great man?

ROSAURA.   So great, I dare not tell you who he is.
I fear to lose your favour.

CLOTALDO.   No, you'd win it
If you would trust me.

ROSAURA.   No, I dare not tell you.

CLOTALDO.   If only I could find out who he is.
Tell me his name. I am your friend. You
      need me.

ROSAURA.   I trust you. You shall know my enemy
Is great Astolfo, Duke of Muscovy.

CLARION *(aside).*
      Why, this is worse than I thought possible.
I must learn more of this. Let us examine
This carefully. You are a Muscovite.
Therefore Astolfo is your natural lord.
And therefore he cannot have wronged your
      honour.
Quench this mad ardour.

ROSAURA.   Though he is my prince,
He's wronged me.

CLOTALDO.   No, a prince can do no wrong,
Not even if he struck you in the face.

ROSAURA.   My wrong was worse than that.

CLOTALDO.   Then tell it to me.

ROSAURA.   I am not what I seem,
This is show, disguise, a costume.
My name is Rosaura.
(Lets down her hair.)
I had a noble mother
In the court of Muscovy.
A deceiver wooed and won her.

I do not know his name
For she would never tell me,
But I think he was valiant
Because I sometimes feel
His courage in myself.
He told her the old story:
He'd be true to her,
He would marry her.
But one day he left her:
She was too low-born
For his nobility.
From this loose knot
I came into the world,
And so in time her tale
Was told again in me.
Astolfo is the man
Who despoiled my honour.
He swore he'd marry me
And for a little while
I thought I was happy.
Suddenly he left.
He came here to Poland
To marry his Estrella.
As a star first joined us
So a star destroyed us.
I wept within.
I was mocked,
I was angry,
I was mad,
I was dead,
I was...me...
Babel...Muddle...Hell.

Pain is felt, not words
But my mother understood.
When you know the person
To whom you tell your weakness
Has been weak herself,
It's as if you are both lost
In the same strange country.
That is a comfort.
She said, "Go to Poland,
Either make him marry you
Or kill him. Kill him with
Your father's sword."
I swore that.

She dressed me as a man
And said, "Show this sword
To the noblemen in Poland,
One of them will know it
And be kind to you
Because you are his child."

I want to meet my father
And tell him how I hate him.
It is because of him
That my Astolfo left me.
He said he could not marry
A girl who had no father
And did not know his name.
Hate is a clear thing.
Though I am in the darkness
I am clear about my father.

CLOTALDO *(aside).*

> O what a maze. I don't know what to do.
> My honour's gored. Astolfo's powerful.
> He is my overlord, she just a woman.
> She must not know yet that I am her father,
> For then she would compel me to avenge her.
> That is our code. Besides she loves me now.
> That's sweet to me. Best leave it as it is.
> I don't know what to do or what to say,
> Best to say nothing till I find my way.

ROSAURA.

> Why do I feel such trust and fondness for you?
> I think it is because you are kind and gentle.
> Why are you silent?

CLOTALDO.

> You have sworn two oaths;
> One of revenge and blood and one to win
> Your love Astolfo. These oaths are at odds.
> I think that is because you do not know
> Whether you love or hate him.

ROSAURA.

> Both.

CLOTALDO.

> That's common.
> But I believe your oaths are dreams, Rosaura.
> You cannot marry one of such high blood.
> You must accept that.

ROSAURA.

> I have tried to do so.
> I locked my rage within but it will out.
> Damn his fine phrases, damn his gentle
> smiling.

Damn his sweet kisses, his fumblings and
   his fondlings.
I'll cut his lying throat. How dare he leave me?

CLOTALDO.   You are violent because you have been hurt,
But Time will mend that. For the good of
   Poland
The Duke must wed Estrella. He must do it.

ROSAURA.   I will prevent him.

CLOTALDO.   How?

ROSAURA.   I do not know.

CLOTALDO.   Do you still hope to win his love again?

ROSAURA.   I cannot tell.

CLOTALDO.   Well, you will never win him
Unless you put a dress on.

ROSAURA.   I'll not do that.

CLOTALDO.   You must. As you are now you are immodest,
Unnatural, and, which is worst, unreal.
You are very fair.

ROSAURA.   My hair is foul and matted.

CLOTALDO.   There, you are a woman.

ROSAURA.   I will put a dress on
                        But I will keep my oath.

CLOTALDO.   I don't believe you.

ROSAURA.   The only man I'll marry is Astolfo.

CLOTALDO.   We will speak further. For the present time
                Since you are unhappy it's not good for you
                To be alone. Therefore I will contrive
                That you shall serve Estrella.

ROSAURA.   I can't do that.

CLOTALDO.   We often think we cannot when we can,
                And what we think we can we often cannot.

ROSAURA.   You must not make me break my oath
                Or go against my honour.

CLOTALDO.   We'll speak further.
                I must attend the King on some great purpose.
                Go in Rosaura, and put on a dress.
                *(Exit CLOTALDO. ROSAURA takes off the
                rest of her disguise. As she does so she sings.)*

ROSAURA.   Dreamed I was the lover
                Of a beautiful thief
                But when I woke up
                I was a shipwreck on a reef.
                Dreamed that I was happy
                Or so it seemed to seem.

My lover smiled
Just like a clown in a dream.

A clown in a dream,
A clown in a dream
I had a dream
I was a clown in a dream.
A clown in a dream
Falling upside down,
And when I woke up,
I was a dream in a clown.
(Exit ROSAURA.)

END OF ACT ONE

ACT TWO

(Enter KING BASILIO and CLOTALDO.)

CLOTALDO.   Your orders, sire, have all been carried out.

BASILIO.   Tell me, Clotaldo.

CLOTALDO.   I went back to the tower
And had a pleasant sleeping draft prepared;
A blend of certain rare and powerful herbs,
Whose secret strength lays waste the human
    mind
So that the victim becomes numb to pain,
And at the last is like a living corpse.

BASILIO.   Sweet medicine is so full of Nature's secrets
That there's no plant nor animal nor stone
That does not have rare powers or properties.
For if the matchless malice of mankind
Can find a thousand poisons, is it strange
That violent drugs, if they be checked and
    tempered,
Can bring us sleep, unto death? It's
palpable.

CLOTALDO.   I took this drink down to the Prince's cell
And talked a little with him of the arts

38

And sciences, which he had learned from birds,
From beasts and fishes, mountains and clouds
   and me.
To raise his spirits to your enterprise
I made him watch a fiery-feathered eagle,
Flying through tree-tall flames of gold and
   white,
Winging beyond the clouded, lower skies,
Soaring up high into the land of the sun.
Until he turned into a shooting star,
A feathered ray of streaming gilded light.
I praised that bright adventurer and said,
"The eagle is the King of all the birds,
The undisputed lord." This image spurred him
To speak of sovereignty. Ambitiously
And proudly too his heart began to stir
Heroically. He said: "It is amazing
Within the airy Kingdom of the birds
One bird holds sway. So many citizens
And yet they all seem happy to obey.
But I'm a subject through some fault of birth,
And, were I free, I never could become
Subject to any man on earth."

BASILIO.   So, he was roused.

CLOTALDO.   And so I thought it good
To offer him the potion, and he took it.
No sooner had it trickled down his throat
Than he turned grey as lead. If I'd not known
The drug's effects I'd have supposed him dead.
We brought him to your room, to your own
   bed.

When he awakes they'll clothe him in your
   robes
And serve him as they'd serve Your Majesty.

BASILIO.   You have done well, Clotaldo. Now all is ready.

CLOTALDO.   Your Highness, if my long obedient years
Have earned, forgive me, any kind of pay,
Will you explain why you have had the Prince
Brought to the palace in this curious way?

BASILIO.   Your curiosity is just, Clotaldo.
The stars, it is the stars above that threaten
Innumerable tragedies of blood.
I want to test them, yes, test out heaven.
I must discover if his destiny
(However scientifically correct)
May not in fact be slightly mitigated
Or even conquered. I believe a man
Is master of his stars. I wish to try him.
I mean to tell him that he is my son
That I may know his nature. You'll ask why
He was brought here asleep. I'll answer that.
If he should learn today that he's my son
And if he then proves cruel and so tomorrow
Awakes in prison, will he not despair?
Therefore I have contrived a kind of ease.
I'll make him think that it is all a dream.
Thus I'll discover his true character,
For he will act by instinct when he wakes.
And, if he fails he'll have some consolation;
For if one day he's worshipped as a King,
The next flung back into his dungeon den,

He will be able to believe he dreamed it.
And that's a useful, realistic creed:
To live life is a dream indeed.

CLOTALDO.   I believe you are mistaken, sire,
To embark on this experiment.
But as the subject is awake
There's no time now for argument.

BASILIO.   I will withdraw. Stay here: you are his tutor.
Tell him the truth. Don't let him be
    bewildered
But help him clear his mind.

CLOTALDO.   Am I to tell him
Everything?

BASILIO.   Yes, for if he knows the truth
He may succeed and pass the test I've set
him.
I'll send the Duke and Princess to him also,
So all the court shall shortly test my son.
A danger known is often not a danger,
And so it will be with Sigismund.
(Exit BASILIO.)

(Enter CLARION in court livery.)

CLARION.   I've come to see King Basil's play.
To get in his theatre I've had to pay:
One glass of beer to a growling guard,
Two chops to the dogs in the Palace yard,

Three rings to a chambermaid—real
   imitation—
In exchange for some curious information.
Four tots of rum and a barrel of beer
To a royal red-nosed halberdier.
Five silk gowns, ornate and oriental
To a lady-in-waiting who's sentimental.
That's what I paid, but what have I bought?
An under-flunkey's position at court.
Where I am guaranteed a ringside view
Of the Royal Circus of How D'Ye Do,
With performing Princesses, Kings who eat
   fire,
And a Prince walking along the High Wire.

CLOTALDO.   Good morning, Clarion,
What is the news?
New clothes I see,
But rather strange shoes.

CLARION.   Now you've agreed
To avenge her offences,
My mistress Rosaura
Has come to her senses.
You've done so much
To relieve her distress
That she's even put on
A beautiful dress.

CLOTALDO.   I'm glad. Those clothes
Put her sex to shame.

CLARION.   On top of all that

She's changed her name
To the lady Astraea.
She says she's your niece,
And she's landed a job,
Wonders never cease,
As a lady-in-waiting
To Princess Estrella,
(Which she couldn't have done
If she'd stayed as a feller).

CLOTALDO.   And how does your life
              As a court clown feel?

CLARION.   I'm desperate, sir,
              I long for a meal.
              A six-course dinner
              Is what I deserve
              But nobody feeds me.
              I've no one to serve.

CLOTALDO.   Then be my servant,
              Though the fare is frugal.

CLARION.   I am your slave, sir.

CLOTALDO.   Then don't blow that bugle.

CLARION.   I'm full of joy
              And I'll learn to diet.

CLOTALDO.   But first you must learn
              To try to be quiet.

(Music.)
Ah, here he comes in princely splendour.

CLARION.   Who?

CLOTALDO.   Prince Sigismund, and his royal retinue.

(SIGISMUND enters, carried on a litter by SERVANTS. He wakes up. They help to dress him as he speaks.)

SIGISMUND.   Stars above...what's all this brightness?
                 Stars above...am I in a vision?
                 Sigismund, waking in an amazing bed,
                 Flowing with softnesses and shining...
                 Sigismund, clothed in robes as light
                 As sunset clouds and shining...
                 Sigismund, carried down sunny corridors
                 By silent servants, eyes and faces shining...
                 This isn't a dream. I know I am awake.
                 It doesn't make sense, but it's joy.
                 I am as I thought I never would be:
                 My chains are gone. Today I'm free.

1ST SERVANT. How sad he is.

2ND SERVANT.   And wouldn't you be sad
                 If you were him?

CLARION.   I wouldn't be.

2ND SERVANT.   What, him?

CLARION.   No, sad.

2ND SERVANT. And yet who would change places with him?

CLARION.   Me, for a start.

2ND SERVANT.   We'd better speak to him.

1ST SERVANT. Will you be pleased to hear the Palace choir?

SIGISMUND.   No singing. No.

2ND SERVANT.   For your delight we planned
                    Some songs.

SIGISMUND.   I want a military band.
                    (Fanfare.)
                    This sound is wondrous to my ears:
                    Now I throw off all doubts and fears.

CLOTALDO.   Your highness, my dear lord,
                    I kiss your hand and say
                    I'm proud that I may humbly
                    Pay homage thus today.

SIGISMUND.   It is Clotaldo. What's his mind, his meaning?
                    In prison he tormented me but now
                    He treats me with respect. What's happening?

CLOTALDO.   I understand your wonderment.
                    In a world where all is strange,
                    Your mind is full of doubts and fears
                    Because of this sudden change.
                    But I can soothe away all doubts
                    And beat all terrors down.

I'm charged to tell you that you are
Heir to the Polish Crown.
You have been kept away from men
Because astrology
Predicted that your rule as King
Would prove a tyranny.
You have been brought here to defy
What the stars relate,
For the man who is magnanimous
Can triumph over fate.
While you were unconscious
You were brought here to this place.
The King, your father, will tell you the rest
Of your story, face to face.

SIGISMUND.   Traitor: one who betrays.
Traitor, you are my traitor.
Now I know who I am,
I am full of pride.
Because of what I am,
I am full of power.
Traitor to Poland, traitor,
Hiding me away
Like a dirty secret
Traitor to me, Sigismund,
Your prisoner, your prince...

CLOTALDO. My lord.

SIGISMUND.   Savage to me and servile to the King.
Therefore the law, the King and I condemn
     you
To death. I'll execute you with these hands.

1ST SERVANT. My lord...

2ND SERVANT.   Your highness...

3RD SERVANT.   Sir...

CLOTALDO.   My lord...

SIGISMUND.   Out of my way. Nobody stops me, no one.
Out of my way, by God, or I will throw you
Out of that window down into the lake.

CLARION.   It's a dark lake.

1ST SERVANT.   Go, sir.

2ND SERVANT.   You'd better go.

CLOTALDO.   I pity you. How powerful you seem
But you may find you're acting in a dream.
(Exit CLOTALDO.)

2ND SERVANT. Consider, sir...

SIGISMUND.   Get out of here.

2ND SERVANT. He only obeyed his King.

SIGISMUND.   He should have refused. I was his Prince.
To lock me away was an unjust thing.

2ND SERVANT. It wasn't for him but the King to decide
Right from wrong and white from black.

SIGISMUND.   You must dislike yourself very much
To risk answering me back.

CLARION.   The Prince is right and you are wrong.

2ND SERVANT. And who asked you to say?

CLARION.   Poland's a free country, isn't it?

1ST SERVANT. Who are you, anyway?

CLARION.   I'm the world champion busy-body.
I've a finger in every pie.
I could kill you two birds
With one bush if I liked
But I've bigger fish to fry.

SIGISMUND.   I know you. You're Clarion the Clown.

CLARION.   Local vodka. Chuck it down.
(CLARION passes SIGISMUND the bottle.)

SIGISMUND *(drinks)*.
I like you,
Clarion the Clown.
You please me,
You're the only one
I like out of all these.

CLARION.   Where pleasing's to be done,
It pleases me to please.

(Enter ASTOLFO. He leaves his hat on.)

ASTOLFO. This is a happy day, most noble prince:
This is the day when you, the sun of Poland,
Must rise and fill the sky and shed your
    brightness
On our horizons like the blushful dawn,
For you have risen like the sunrise does
Above the darkness of the dusky mountains.
O may the lovely laurels on your brow,
These late adornments, flourish long upon
    you
And never wither.

SIGISMUND.   God be with you, sir.

ASTOLFO. Sir, I forgive you that you do not know me
And do not give me honour when it's due.
I am Astolfo, Duke of Muscovy,
And we are cousins. You and I are equals.

1ST SERVANT. Remember, your grace, his highness was
    brought
Up in the mountains, not in the court.

2ND SERVANT. The Duke, my lord, is an aristocrat.

SIGISMUND. He bores me. And he won't take off his hat.

1ST SERVANT. His rank allows that.

2ND SERVANT.   More respect is due.

SIGISMUND. To me, not him. I'm getting tired of you.

(Enter ESTRELLA.)

ESTRELLA.   Sir, welcome to the throne which longs for
                  you
              And gratefully receives you. May you reign,
              Confounding fate, and live a thousand
              years.

SIGISMUND.   Clarion, who is she? Who is this human
                  goddess?

1ST SERVANT. Princess Estrella, sir.

2ND SERVANT.   She is your cousin.

SIGISMUND.   Estrella? That's a star, but I should say
              She is the sun. I thank you for your kindness.
              Queen of the skies, you are the waking
                  daylight.
              You could add brightness to the morning star
              And light the heavens. When you rise at
                  morning
              There's nothing left for the dull sun to do.
              O let me kiss your hand, that snow-pure cup
              From which the gentle breeze drinks
                  whiteness up.

ESTRELLA.   Eloquent Prince, I did not mean...

ASTOLFO.   He must not touch her.

2ND SERVANT.   I'll intervene.

1ST SERVANT. Astolfo's angry.

2ND SERVANT.   Sir, is not your greeting
Too ardent and too rough for a first meeting?

SIGISMUND.   Didn't I say keep out of my way?
Didn't I say keep out of my sight?
The coach is coming. Keep off the highway.

2ND SERVANT. You have just said that rulers must
Always cleave to what is just.

SIGISMUND.   I also said, for Jesus' sake,
That I would throw you in the lake.

2ND SERVANT. You couldn't, sire, a man of my standing...

SIGISMUND.   O couldn't I?

ESTRELLA.   Stop him!

SIGISMUND.   Happy landings!
(*Lifts him in his arms and rushes out.*)

ASTOLFO.   Sweet, fetch the King.

ESTRELLA.   I'll ask him to hurry.

CLARION.   Tell him I'm here and not to worry.

(*Exit ESTRELLA. Re-enter SIGISMUND.*)

SIGISMUND.　　　Your standing notwithstanding, slave.
　　　　　　　　Rest your bones in that chilly grave.

ASTOLFO.　　　　Restrain yourself, my lord: the difference
　　　　　　　　Between a beast and man should be as great
　　　　　　　　As that between a mountain and a palace.

SIGISMUND.　　　Astolfo, if you carry on
　　　　　　　　Giving advice like that,
　　　　　　　　You'll find you have no stupid head
　　　　　　　　On which to put your stupid hat.

(Exit ASTOLFO. Enter KING BASILIO.)

BASILIO.　　　　What have you done?

SIGISMUND.　　　　　　　　　　　Nothing much. I taught a
　　　　　　　　Slave a lesson. Dropped him in the water.
　　　　　　　　(Pause.)
　　　　　　　　Are you my father?

BASILIO.　　　　I am and love you...

SIGISMUND.　　　　　　　　　　No, you've done me wrong.

BASILIO.　　　　You have done wrong, my son. What, take
　　　　　　　　　a life
　　　　　　　　The very first day that you taste your
　　　　　　　　　freedom?

SIGISMUND.　　　He said I couldn't do it, so I did.

BASILIO.　　　　This grieves me, Prince. Be more intelligent.

I hoped to find a new, wise, prudent man
Triumphing over destiny and the stars.
Instead I find a brutal murderer.
How can I give you love? How can I open
My arms to yours? They are a killer's arms.
I thought to embrace you with a father's
   love.
But now you'll understand if I prefer
To avoid the arms of a murderer.

SIGISMUND.   I do not want your love or your embraces.
You are a cruel father. You have kept me
Away from you and reared me like a beast.
You have denied my human dignity,
So I feel nothing for you, father. Nothing.

BASILIO.   I gave you life. I wish I never had.

SIGISMUND.   And if you hadn't, I'd have no complaints.
You gave me life and then wrenched it away.
To give is blessed but give and take away
Is twisted work.

BASILIO.   Is that the thanks I get
For making a poor prisoner a Prince?

SIGISMUND.   What have you given me that was not mine?
You took my free will, chained it to the wall,
And now you are an old, weak dying King,
And you must leave me everything. It's mine.
Poland is mine. There's nothing that I owe
   you.
You owe me life and happiness and freedom.

You should be thanking me I do not force
    you
To pay your debt.

BASILIO.   Look on him, everyone:
See how the stars have kept their promises.
See, see how cruel and arrogant he is.
My son, I warn you, be more kind, more
    gentle,
More humble. That is good advice to take:
Perhaps you only dream that you're awake.

SIGISMUND.   Is this a dream? I feel, I hear, I touch.
I know what I have been and what I am.
You may regret it but you can't undo it.
For I am what I am. What's done is done.
I am half-man, half-beast. I'm not your son.

(ALL exit. Enter ROSAURA dressed in white.)

ROSAURA.   Now Sigismund's a prince and I a lady.
O it is sweet to wear a dress again.
I'm full of joy. Astolfo loves me still.
I saw him come to visit his Estrella
And he still wears my picture. He'd not do
    that
Unless he loved me. I will work on him.
There's time enough to think upon revenge.
Am I not fair? Am I not painted fine?
As I am now I'm fit to wed a King.
A Duke is easy, I will woo and win him.
Clotaldo says I must not speak to him.
I owe him much and therefore should obey.

And yet I will not. I am strong today
Because I find I'm fairer than Estrella.
What jewel's best to wear? Or this? Or this?
I'll find out ways to make myself more fine.
When I was man my heart was torn by strife.
But now I'm woman I may yet be wife.
(*She puts on various jewels.*)

(*Enter SIGISMUND.*)

SIGISMUND.   The world is all as I thought it would be.
Through books and pictures I foresaw it all.
But if I had to wonder at one thing
In this new world, I'd wonder at a woman
And at her beauty. Once in some old book
I read that of all things in God's creation
Man was God's loveliest and noblest work
Because a man is like a little world.
But I believe that woman is the noblest,
For she's a little heaven and more lovely...
And far more so, if she's the one I look on.

ROSAURA (*sees SIGISMUND*).
It is the prince. I'll leave him.

SIGISMUND.   Wait, woman, listen. Tell me who you are.

ROSAURA.   I think, but am not sure, that I have seen you.

SIGISMUND.   I think I've seen your beauty once before.

ROSAURA.   I've seen your rage and sorrow in your prison.

SIGISMUND.   Who are you? You are fair. I've found my
        life.

ROSAURA.   I'm a poor lady in Estrella's train.

SIGISMUND.   No, do not say that. Say you are the sun
        And that Estrella is a petty star
        Who gets her splendour from your borrowed
          flame.
        O I have seen the kingdom of the flowers
        Where every odour is and every hue,
        And where the rose is goddess o'er the rest
        And queen because she is most beautiful.
        And I have seen a world of precious gems
        Deep in the dark academy of the mines,
        And how the rest all hail the diamond
        And call it emperor for its radiance.
        And I have seen up in the courts of heaven,
        High in the lovely empire of the stars,
        The morning star in royal pre-eminence.
        And I have seen how in the very spheres
        The sun, that is the oracle of day,
        Calls up the planets to his parliament
        And plays the speaker. If among all these,
        The flowers, the mines, the firmament, the
          planets,
        The fairest is exalted, how can I
        Serve one who is less beautiful than you,
        Who are for loveliness and excellence
        The peer of roses, diamonds, sun and stars?

(Enter CLOTALDO, unseen.)

CLOTALDO *(aside).*

> I educated him. It's up to me
> To advise the boy. But first I'll wait and see.

ROSAURA.

> My lord, I'm honoured by your eloquence
> But I'm lost for words. My reply is silence.

SIGISMUND.

> Your body speaks and everything about you.
> You shine. O do not leave me in the dark.

ROSAURA.

> I beg your leave to go...

SIGISMUND.

>   Stay where you are.
> You do not beg my leave, you simply take it.

ROSAURA.

> If you won't give it I am bound to take it.

SIGISMUND.

> Well then, you'll see the dark side of my
>   passion,
> The Beast-man. Say, why are you dressed
>   so fine
> Unless you mean to set a man on fire?

ROSAURA.

> I did not dress to please you.

SIGISMUND.

>   But you do.
> You've made yourself a lure and flame to
>   men.

ROSAURA.

> I have not...

SIGISMUND.

>   Come, resistance poisons patience.

I've seen you thus, and seen you as a man.
Now I will see you as you truly are.

ROSAURA.   You would not dare. You will respect my
                honour.

SIGISMUND.   We'll see. You'll make me try it, though
                  I am
                Afraid of you because you are so fair.
                I must know whether I can love or not.
                I want to conquer the impossible.
                Today I threw a man over that balcony
                Down into the black lake. I did it, lady,
                Because he said I couldn't. Now I'll throw
                Your chastity out of the window after.
                (*He throws her on the bed and starts to tear
                her clothes off.*)

CLOTALDO (*aside*).
                It is not good that he should thus divest him,
                And yet the King has said that we must test
                  him.

ROSAURA.   The stars were right. They spoke the truth.
                  I see
                You'll be a tyrant. You will fill up Poland
                With riot, slaughter, treachery and crime.
                What else can be expected of a creature
                As barbarous, inhuman and relentless,
                As is a beast that is brought up with beasts?

CLOTALDO (*aside*).

> I've waited long enough and I have seen
> What he intends. I'd better intervene.

SIGISMUND.   I've tried to speak to you with gentleness
> Because I hoped you would be kind to me,
> But since you are so sure I am a beast,
> I'll prove I am one.

CLOTALDO.   Pardon me, my lord...

SIGISMUND.   How did you get in here?

CLOTALDO.   I...

SIGISMUND.   Go away.

ROSAURA.   I'm lost. Wait, listen...

SIGISMUND.   No, I am a tyrant.
> I am the Beast-man.

CLOTALDO.   Wait, my lord. Be careful.

SIGISMUND.   Doddering old fool, how dare you interrupt?

CLOTALDO.   I heard your voice raised angrily
> And wanted, Prince, to say:
> Try to be mild and humble
> And show gentleness today,
> Or you may wake to find your power
> Has melted, like a dream away.

SIGISMUND.　　　Now I will kill you. We'll soon see
　　　　　　　　If this is a dream or reality.

CLOTALDO (*kneels and grabs hold of SIGISMUND*).
　　　　　　　　I mean to live.

SIGISMUND.　　　　　　　Let go.

CLOTALDO.　　　　　　　　　　I'll not let go.
　　　　　　　　I know you mean to throw me in the lake.

ROSAURA.　　　For God's sake help.

SIGISMUND.　　　　　　　　　Old fool, I say, let go.
　　　　　　　　Or I will crush you in my arms to death.

ROSAURA.　　　Quickly, come quickly! Clotaldo's being
　　　　　　　　murdered.

　　(Exit ROSAURA. Enter ASTOLFO.)

ASTOLFO.　　　Stay, noble prince.
　　　　　　　　What, stain an old man's blood? You will
　　　　　　　　　not do that.

SIGISMUND.　　　If blood is in his dusty veins, I will.

ASTOLFO.　　　I'll answer for his life.

SIGISMUND.　　　　　　　　You'll answer, will you?
　　　　　　　　You have insulted me. Now I shall kill you.

ASTOLFO.　　　Then I will draw in self-defence, my lord,

And that's no treason.
(They fight.)

CLOTALDO *(to ASTOLFO).*   Do not hurt him, sire.

(Enter BASILIO, ESTRELLA, SERVANTS and CLARION.)

BASILIO.   What, swords?

ESTRELLA.   Astolfo, hold.

BASILIO.   Hold, both of you.
What is it?

ASTOLFO.   Nothing. You are here: it's over.
(ASTOLFO sheathes his sword.)
No man will draw his sword before his King.

SIGISMUND.   You should have said you drew against your
King.

CLOTALDO.   Humour him, sire. Do it all gently.

CLARION.   What was the cause? Explain it, pray.

SIGISMUND.   I wanted to make love to a lady
But those old bones appeared.
I wanted to kill that old fool
But the Cossack interfered.

BASILIO.   What, do you not respect a lady's honour?
Don't you respect this good old man's grey
hair?

CLOTALDO.   Her honour's untarnished. So is my grey hair.

SIGISMUND.   I was brought up with horror and grey air.
                   I'm getting ready for the day
                   When I'll squash your Royal honour
                   Under my boots and use your silver beard
                   As a mat to wipe my feet on.

BASILIO.   Wild, monstrous, rash. O you are barbarous.

SIGISMUND.   You brought me up like a rat in a box
                   But I'll be revenged on you, Grizzly-locks.

BASILIO.   Now I am sure the cruel stars spoke true.
                   All of you, mark him, mark his insolence.
                   You have all heard him. He would be
                      revenged.
                   No, Sigismund, my son, before that happens,
                   You'll sleep again where you slept
                      yesterday.

(BASILIO signals to the SERVANTS. They seize SIGIS-
MUND and CLARION. BASILIO pours a potion into
SIGISMUND's mouth. He falls asleep.)

                   Now you shall think that everything which
                      passed
                   Here in the palace on your happy day,
                   Like all good things on earth, was so much
                      dreaming.
                   Clotaldo, take him back into the mountains.
                   Estrella and the Duke shall reign in Poland.
                   (Exeunt.)

(Enter ASTOLFO and ESTRELLA.)

ASTOLFO.
I see, Estrella, that the stars spoke true:
Take Sigismund and myself, for we were
    born
Under two signs. For him there was foretold
A life of crime and it has come to pass;
But for my part, when I first saw your eyes
They were as stars, my stars, for then they
    spoke
To me of bliss and fame and great
    possessions.
Is it not so? Or are the fickle stars
True only when they tell of evil things?

ESTRELLA.
I do not doubt that these fine words of yours
Are finely meant, but are they meant for me?
What of the woman whose bewitching
    picture
You wore about your neck when we first
    met?
I think it must be so. These compliments
Belong to her, so go and take them to her,
And she'll reward you for your gentleness.
Kind words and courtesies to other women
Are scarcely current in the Court of Love.

ASTOLFO.
I never wear that portrait now. It chokes me.
I have made room for you and for your
    beauty.
For where Estrella is there are no shadows,
As there are no stars by the noonday sun.
I'll fetch the picture, madam.

(Exit ESTRELLA.)

                    Fair Rosaura,
Forgive me now. I know too well that I
Do ill in this, but when a man or woman
Is separated from the one they love,
They rarely keep their faiths. And so with me.
I'll get the portrait.
(Exit ASTOLFO.)

(Re-enter ESTRELLA.)

ESTRELLA.   O how we act and do not show our minds.
I know he does not love me but he woos
In policy. And I in likewise act
And now seem cold. That's likewise policy,
For I believe that is the way to win him.

(Enter ROSAURA, demurely dressed.)

ROSAURA *(aside).*
           I changed my dress because I thought it
           safer.

ESTRELLA.   Astraea...

ROSAURA.   Yes, my lady?

ESTRELLA.   I am glad
That you have come. I have a secret for you.

ROSAURA.   You honour me and I obey you, madam.

ESTRELLA.   I have not known you long and yet I trust you.
I want to share my inmost mind with you.

ROSAURA.   I am your slave.

ESTRELLA.   Then as you know, Astolfo,
Who is my cousin, means to marry me,
Which it is hoped, will cancel much
        misfortune
With one great joy. But though I dote on him
I dare not show it. Something troubles me.
When he arrived in Poland he was wearing
A portrait of a lady round his neck.
I asked him if he loved her. He denied it.
He's gone to fetch it but I'd be embarrassed
To take it from him. You stay here instead,
And when he comes ask him to give it to you.
(Exit ESTRELLA.)

ROSAURA.   What woman is there wise and calm enough
To know what she should do if she was I?
When I was man, I wished I was a woman,
But now I am I wish I was a man.
O what a pickle and a maze I'm in:
I curse the hour that I was born feminine.
I'm sworn to serve Estrella and to get
My picture back. I'm sworn to obey Clotaldo
Who saved my life. He said I must not woo
Astolfo, yet I'm sworn to or to kill him.
Nor am I now suited to please the man.
I fear that I am ugly, dull and nasty.
I am the fool of love. What shall I do?
I can't pretend, I. When Astolfo comes,

However much I plan and I prepare
I'll do...O God, I don't know what I'll do.

(Enter ASTOLFO.)

ASTOLFO.   Here is the portrait, madam...
                Good God!

ROSAURA.   What troubles you?
                Why do you stare at my face?

ASTOLFO.   To see you in this place.
                Rosaura...

ROSAURA.   I am sorry, sir,
                You're very much mistaken,
                I am called Astraea.
                I'm a lady-in-waiting.
                I am not the noble lady you seek,
                If I may judge by the way you speak.

ASTOLFO.   Do not pretend, Rosaura,
                What if you're called Astraea,
                I love you as Rosaura...

ROSAURA.   I do not understand one word you utter.
                So please, your highness, all that I can say
                Is that Estrella (who may be the star
                Of love itself, since that's Estrella's
                      meaning)
                Told me to wait for you and in her place
                To take a picture which you'd bring for her.
                The lady wants it and I must obey her.

ASTOLFO.   Inform your eyes, they contradict your voice.

                If you uttered lies with perfect control
                I'd look through your eyes and see your soul.

ROSAURA.   I want the picture. That is why I'm here.

ASTOLFO.   Then, if you want to lie like you do,
                Go to the princess and say this, Astraea:
                She asked me for a picture but I prize her
                Too much to send her such a petty gift,
                Instead of that, in love and in devotion,
                I send her now the sweet original.
                Go, take it to her. You are bound to take it
                Wherever you may go.

ROSAURA.   If I return
                With the original and not the copy
                I shall have failed my duty to my mistress.
                I came for the portrait.
                Give me the portrait.
                I must have the portrait.

ASTOLFO.   I will not give it
                And you cannot take it.

ROSAURA.   I'll tear it from you.
                You devil. Let go.
                (She tries to seize it.)

ASTOLFO.   What use is that?

ROSAURA.   By God,

I will not let it fall
Into another woman's hands.

ASTOLFO.   You admit you're Rosaura.
You said that you'd give it
Back to your mistress.

ROSAURA.   I do not care what I said.

ASTOLFO.   You're angry.

ROSAURA.   You're base.

ASTOLFO.   That's enough. You are mine.

ROSAURA.   I am not, you lie.
You bully, you liar.
(She grabs the picture again.)

(Enter ESTRELLA.)

ESTRELLA.   Astraea. Astolfo.
What is this?

ASTOLFO.   Estrella.

ROSAURA *(aside)*.
                    Love, grant me all your cunning
So I can get the picture.
My lady, I'll explain.

ASTOLFO.   Now what's her plan?

ROSAURA.   Madam, you told me to wait
                For Astolfo to bring a portrait.
                I was day-dreaming:
                You know the way. I remembered
                A portrait of my own.
                I opened it but dropped it.
                Then Astolfo came.
                He would not give me his
                But picked up mine instead
                And would not give it back.
                I pleaded but he held on,
                So I tried to take it from him.
                There it is, in his hand.
                It's mine. It looks like mine.

ESTRELLA.   Astolfo, give it to me.

ASTOLFO.   Madam...

ESTRELLA.   It flatters you:
                There is a calm about it.

ROSAURA.   Yes, it's my portrait.

ESTRELLA.   I do not doubt it.

ROSAURA.   Then you should order him
                To give you the other one.

ESTRELLA.   Take your own and go.

ROSAURA *(aside).*
> Now I've got mine back
> I'll watch and see what happens.

ASTOLFO.   Madam, I can explain…

ESTRELLA.   Give me the picture which you promised me.
> Although I hope that I shall never see you
> Or speak to you again, I do not want it
> To stay in your hands. I see I was foolish
> To ask for it. So give it back again.

ASTOLFO.   Lovely Estrella, I do not know how
> I can return the portrait.

ESTRELLA.   Do not try.
> Flirt with my servant: so much for you love.
> I don't want your picture. Whatever you do
> It would only remind me I begged it of you.
> *(Exit ESTRELLA.)*

ASTOLFO.   Estrella, listen!
> Damn you, Rosaura. Everything was fine
> Till you arrived in Poland. You'll destroy
> me.
> My hopes hang on this marriage. If it fails
> I'll tear Rosaura's eyes out with my nails.

ROSAURA *(comes forward).*
> Then tear them out. I will be glad of it.

ASTOLFO.   Rosaura, you have done much mischief to me.

ROSAURA.   Astolfo, you have done much mischief to me.

ASTOLFO.   That's past. What you've just done will
                    undo Poland.
                You see how Sigismund's unfit to reign.

ROSAURA.   You're not fit either. You have broke your
                    oath.

ASTOLFO.   Yes, I did as the world does.

ROSAURA.   Than you're base
                As mean men are.

ASTOLFO.   I could not marry you
                (I see that I must spell it out again)
                Because you do not know who was your
                    father.
                You know that is our law, our code, our
                    custom.
                I will not, cannot go against my honour.

ROSAURA.   You went against it when you mangled mine.

ASTOLFO.   It's true I did you wrong...

ROSAURA.   Why then,

ASTOLFO.   No, listen.
                You do wrong now to make so much of it.
                Love does not last. It fades. To cling to it
                When it is done is tedious and foolish.
                I know that you love to torment yourself:

> You hug your woes just as your mother did.
> That's why you serve Estrella and that's why
> You tried to get me to give up your picture.

ROSAURA.   You're full of reasons but what's in your
> heart?
> Tell me one thing.

ASTOLFO.   What?

ROSAURA.   Do you love Estrella?

ASTOLFO.   I will not tell you. If I said I did
> You'd plague yourself, and if I said I did not
> You'd go on clinging to your hopes and
> dreams.

ROSAURA.   To live in doubt's a plague.

ASTOLFO.   That's how you are.
> You twist and turn all that I say to you.
> That is your woman's nature.

ROSAURA.   You are so vile.
> You twist and turn, not I. That's your man's
> nature.
> You broke your oath but I will not break
> mine.

ASTOLFO.   What have you sworn?

ROSAURA.   Either to marry you
> Or kill you. Why do you laugh?

ASTOLFO.   You can do neither.

ROSAURA.   Let time tell that.

ASTOLFO.   No, let time tell it now.
I challenge you. Here is my dagger. Use it.

ROSAURA.   I will not kill you with a mean man's weapon.
I am sworn to slay you with my father's
    sword.

ASTOLFO.   Well, keep your oath.

ROSAURA.   I do not have it with me.

ASTOLFO.   Fetch it and I will wait. Why, it's apparent
You cannot do it. Now I know that I
Did right when I forsook you, for I see
You are not of noble blood. Do not reproach
    me
That I'm forsworn, for you are now as I am.
Therefore have done, go home to Muscovy,
Forget what's past and get yourself a husband,
And talk no more of vengeance, oaths and
    honour.
(*Aside.*) Some men might say that was quite
    a close call.
But I know about love. There was no risk
    at all.
(*Exit ASTOLFO.*)

ROSAURA.   Alas. I'm worse off than I was before.
O what a fool I was. Alone with him:

I should have wooed him or I should have
  killed him.
All that he said is true. I have no honour.
I am forsworn. I do torment myself.
I am a mingle, I am full of voices
That war in me and buzz inside my head.
I cannot help it. I am as I am.
It cannot be but that I have bad stars.
What shall I do? How shall I find a clearness?
An oath is clear, and I will keep mine yet.
Then, stars, be kind and help me find a way
To kill Astolfo. There's no more to say.
(Exit ROSAURA.)

SCENE TWO

*(CLOTALDO and GUARDS carry in SIGISMUND and
CLARION. They leave SIGISMUND on the floor and chain
him.)*

CLOTALDO.   He has had his day.

1ST GUARD.   Here's his old rusty chain.

CLOTALDO.   His pride has led him back
                Into black night again.
                (Exit CLOTALDO and GUARDS.)

CLARION.   Somnolent, somniferous.
                When the arms of Morpheus
                Give you back to consciousness

You will find your luck
Has drowned in the black lake.
All your pomp is muck:
It was all a fake.
Your life is a game,
A little shadow-play
Lit by death's candle-flame
For one brief day.

(Re-enter GUARDS and CLOTALDO with a candle.)

CLOTALDO.   You talk too much.
    Go, chain him in a cell.

CLARION.   Why me?

CLOTALDO.   You know too much.
    You're a noisy Clarion.

CLARION.   What have I done?
    I ask you? Have I ever tried
    To kill my father or something worse?
    Or tried to rape a Princess?
    Never! Quite the reverse.
    Do I throw servants in the lake?
    Do I get reborn, for God's sake?
    Do I dream? Do I sleep? I do not. So
    Why lock me up?

CLOTALDO.   Because of what you know.

CLARION.   At least make sure

> I'm properly fed
> With plenty to drink.

CLOTALDO (to GUARDS).
> You heard what he said.

(GUARDS take CLARION out. Enter KING BASILIO, cloaked and masked.)

BASILIO.   Clotaldo.

CLOTALDO.   Sire, why have you come disguised?

BASILIO.   It was perhaps unwise but I am curious
> To see what happens now to Sigismund.

CLOTALDO.   Well, there he lies as he did formerly.

BASILIO.   Unlucky Prince. Tragic nativity.

CLOTALDO.   He's restless. He is talking in his sleep.

BASILIO.   What does he dream of now? We'll listen
> to him.

SIGISMUND (in his sleep).
> Princes show mercy when they murder
>> tyrants.
> I'll crush Clotaldo. He'll be old dead meat.
> Where is my father? Let him kiss my feet.

CLOTALDO.   He threatens me with death.

BASILIO.   And me with shame.

SIGISMUND *(in his sleep)*.

     I will be brave, my cue is blood and
        vengeance.
     I'll be revenged upon the King, my father,
     And trample him in dust on this great stage,
     The theatre of the world...
     (Wakes.)   O where am I?
     Light...darkness...Fetters again?
     A slave? What things I've dreamed of...

CLOTALDO *(aside)*.

     I will delude the Prince.
     Time to wake up. Have you slept all day
        long?
     We talked last night of eagles, and I think
     You've slept since then.

SIGISMUND.   I've slept since then...

CLOTALDO.   I've tracked
     An eagle in the air while you were sleeping.

SIGISMUND.   I think that I am still asleep, Clotaldo.
     It must be so, for if the things I saw
     When I was dreaming were so clear and
        bright,
     What I see now must be unreal and
        shadows.

CLOTALDO.   Tell me your dream.

SIGISMUND.　　　　　　　　　　　If it had been a dream
I would not tell it. What I saw, Clotaldo,
I saw indeed, and it was real I saw.
I woke. And then I saw myself, in bed
Soft comforting, the cover sweetly woven

Like springtime meadows in our mountain
　lands,
Cornflower, wild strawberry and lady's
　slipper.
Courtiers knelt and hailed me as their Prince,
And then you told me I was Prince of
　Poland.

CLOTALDO.　And when I told you that, how did you thank
　me?

SIGISMUND.　Not well. I think I tried to kill you twice.
Yes, I was angry and I called you traitor.

CLOTALDO.　Were you so cruel?

SIGISMUND.　　　　　　　　　I thought I saw my father
And hated him. For I was all men's master
And wanted my revenge upon them all,
Except one woman whom I know I loved.
The rest have vanished, but her picture is
Branded upon my mind. She must be real.

　　(Exit BASILIO.)

CLOTALDO (aside).
　　The King has gone. He's moved.

Because we talked a while last night of
   eagles
You dreamed of empires when you went to
   bed.
But you would do well, even in your dreams,
To honour those who care for you each day.
Kindness is never wasted, even in dreams,
And gentleness is never thrown away.
(Exit CLOTALDO.)

SIGISMUND.   Perhaps that's true. Perhaps I should snuff
   out
This flame of rage, this blaze of red ambition.
The time may come when we shall dream
   again.
In this strange world to live's a kind of
   dreaming,
And each of us must dream the thing he is
Till he awakes. The King dreams he's a
   King,
Lives, orders, governs in a royal illusion,
Because his fame is written in the wind.
For every King that rules men in his
   King-dream
Must wake at last in the cold sleep of death.
The rich man dreams his riches which are
   cares,
The poor man dreams his penury and pain,
The man who prospers dreams, the man
   who strives,
The man who hurts men, and the man who's
   hurt,

All dream. So what's this life? A fraud, a
   frenzy,
A trick, a tale, a shadow, an illusion.
And all our life is nothing but a dream.
And what are dreams? They are no more
   than dreamstuff.
And what is real is nothing, and a man
Is nothing neither.
(Snuffs out the candle.)
                It is all a dream.
(Exit SIGISMUND.)

END OF ACT TWO

ACT THREE

SCENE ONE

(Enter CLARION.)

CLARION *(sings)*.

> Lord, I am a drinking man
> With nothing left to lose.
> My quest is for oblivion,
> My weapon is the booze.
> My enemy's reality—
> I dodge her when I can.
> God bless the drinking man...
>
> Lord, I am a drinking man.
> I'm drinking to forget
> Something I remembered
> When my memory was wet.
> O brandy sun, shine down on me
> And give me tippler's tan.
> God bless the drinking man...
>
> Though they've locked me in a cell
> Like Cervantes in the clink,
> I shall manage very well,
> If I have enough to drink.
> I'll swig it from a goblet,
> I'll sip it from a can,
> God bless the drinking man...

> Lord, I am a drinking man
> And when I die of thirst,
> Place me in a champagne vat,
> Totally immersed.
> An after-life of stupor
> Is my religious plan.
> God bless the drinking man...

(Drums. Clamour and banging outside. Enter SOLDIERS.)

1ST SOLDIER. This is the tower. Where is the prisoner?

CLARION.   It must be me that they are looking for.

2ND SOLDIER. He's here.

CLARION.   No, he's not here.

1ST SOLDIER.   Your Majesty.

CLARION.   You must be drunk.

1ST SOLDIER.   You are our rightful prince.

2ND SOLDIER. We want our natural lord.

3RD SOLDIER.   No Muscovite.

2ND SOLDIER. No foreign prince for us. Break off his chains.

CLARION.   It's real. They are not joking. They want me.
               It must be a custom in this curious kingdom
               To make someone a prince here for a day

And then to throw him back in jail again.
And now it's my turn.

3RD SOLDIER. We kiss your feet, sire.

1ST SOLDIER.   Sir, give us your feet.

CLARION.   I can't. I need them. Princes need their feet.

2ND SOLDIER. What is your will, my lord?

CLARION.   What is my will?
          Now I am Prince of Poland
          I'll free all drunks and debtors.
          I'll put the politicians
          Respectfully in fetters.

          I promise to my subjects
          Steaks shall grow on trees
          And a cathedral shall be carved
          From Gorgonzola cheese.

          My kingdom's cows shall give us
          Vodka instead of milk.
          Harlots will pay their clients
          And beggars sleep in silk.

          My policy for Poland
          Is: set the people free.
          And when I say the people,
          I mean people like me.

1ST SOLDIER. We've told the King
                We want no other prince but you to rule us.

CLARION.   Did you not treat my father with respect?

2ND SOLDIER. We spoke out of our loyalty to you.

CLARION.   If you were being loyal then I forgive you.

1ST SOLDIER. Prince Sigismund, come forth and rule your
                kingdom.

CLARION.   That seems to be the name they give to all
                Their player princes.

SOLDIERS.   Long live Sigismund.

(Enter SIGISMUND.)

SIGISMUND.   Who calls on Sigismund?

1ST SOLDIER.   Who is this man?

CLARION.   That is the true prince. I am just a player.
                I abdicate.

1ST SOLDIER.   Which one of you is the prince?

SIGISMUND.   I have been told that I am.

2ND SOLDIER.   Little fool,
                Why did you say you were?

CLARION.   I didn't, you did.
     You Sigismunded me. You are the fool,
     Not I.
     (Exit CLARION.)

1ST SOLDIER.   Enough of this. Prince Sigismund.
     Your father is a clever, cunning man
     But he believes the world's run by the stars.
     He is afraid of prophecies which say
     He will kneel at your feet. Therefore he wants
     To lock you up, deprive you of your rights
     And give them to the Duke of Muscovy.
     And to that end he called a parliament
     And so awoke the people. We know now
     That we already have a native heir
     And do not want a foreigner to rule us,
     Especially a Muscovite. So come with us.
     We all know how to fight. The mountain's
      swarming
     With soldiers, outlaws, peasants, prisoners,
     Who hail you as their King. Then come away
     And seize the crown and sceptre from the
      tyrant.
     (Drums and trumpets.)

SOLDIERS.   Long live King Sigismund.

SIGISMUND.   It sounds again.
     What do you want with me this time, you
      stars?
     Another bubble? Another shadow-play?
     And will it once more vanish in the dark?
     No, not again. No dreaming. I'll not do it.

Ghosts, go away. You all seem to have bodies
And voices, but you have none. You are
　　shadows.
You are like me: you are asleep. You're
　　dream-men.
I will not be the plaything of the stars.
I will not be like some rash almond tree
Which buds too soon so that its pink and
　　white
Shatters like glass in the first ruthless frost
And all its loveliness and light is lost.

1ST SOLDIER. If you believe that we are lying to you,
　　　　　　Look at the mountainside: all those men are
　　　　　　　with us.

2ND SOLDIER. They await your orders.

SIGISMUND.　　　　　　　　　Yes, I see them clearly.
　　　　　I see you clearly too. But once before
　　　　　I saw as clear as that but I was dreaming.

1ST SOLDIER. My lord, they say before a great event
　　　　　　There's some great sign. Your king-dreaming
　　　　　　　was an omen
　　　　　　To make you ready.

2ND SOLDIER.　　　　　　　This event is real.

SIGISMUND.　What are your names?

1ST SOLDIER.　　　　　　We don't have names, my lord.

2ND SOLDIER. We leave our names at home.

3RD SOLDIER.   It's dangerous
            To use real names.

SIGISMUND.   How many of you are there?

1ST SOLDIER. We're numberless.

2ND SOLDIER.   As stars are.

3RD SOLDIER.   You could say
            That we go on forever.

SIGISMUND.   I believe
            You speak the truth and my dream was an
                omen.
            Let us suppose that. But what then? Life's
                brief,
            So let us dream. And yet I know my nature.
            Therefore I must remember as I dream
            I must be politic. Let's all remember
            That we must wake up when we least expect it.
            Since we know that and know that we must
                suffer
            We'll suffer less because we know we shall.

            I will go on. I thank your loyalty.
            I'll free you all from foreign rule in Poland.
            I'll prove the stars spoke true and make my
                father
            Grovel before me...if I don't wake up...

SOLDIERS.   King Sigismund!

(Drums. Enter CLOTALDO.)

CLOTALDO.   Guards! Where are the guards?

SIGISMUND.   It is Clotaldo.

CLOTALDO.   I kiss your feet. I know that I must die.

SIGISMUND.   No. You must be the North Star in my sky.
                 Stand up, Clotaldo, do not be afraid.
                 You must still be my guide and counsellor.

CLOTALDO.   What do you mean?

SIGISMUND.   I mean that I am dreaming.
                 But I would like to act well in my dream.

CLOTALDO.   If doing good is now your game
                 Do not be surprised
                 If I want to do the same.
                 You do not know these men.
                 If you'll wage war against your father
                 How can I be your adviser?
                 He is my King. All I can do
                 Is offer up my life to you.

SIGISMUND.   I am your King. You are a traitor to me.

1ST SOLDIER.   Your fine words are a mockery, Clotaldo.

CLOTALDO.   You are all traitors. Where's your loyalty?

2ND SOLDIER. We are the loyal ones and you are the traitor.

CLOTALDO.   Rebellion is damnation in a subject.

3RD SOLDIER. To be a subject is a true damnation.

CLOTALDO.   You twist my words.

1ST SOLDIER.   You twist reality.

SIGISMUND.   Enough of this.

CLOTALDO.   My lord...

SIGISMUND.   Clotaldo, listen:
              If that is how you feel, go to the King.
              Don't try to tell me what is good or bad,
              I think that each man's honour is his own.
              Farewell. We'll meet in a battle.

CLOTALDO.   You're generous, but if you hope to reign,
              You must remember things may change
              again.
              (Exit CLOTALDO.)

SIGISMUND.   Now to the Palace. Drums and trumpets,
                 sound.
              (Drums and trumpets.)
              Come Zodiac, we go to reign.
              I am as my stars make me.
              If this is real don't let me sleep.
              If I'm asleep, don't wake me.
              What matters is to try

To do what is right.
Then if it is real
Right justifies itself,
And if it is unreal
It does no harm to have
Some credit up in heaven.
It may be useful on the day
That we awake and end the play.
(They go out of the prison.)

SCENE TWO

(Enter ESTRELLA and ROSAURA.)

ESTRELLA.   He picked it up? You did not give it to him?

ROSAURA.   No, madam.

ESTRELLA.   Swear it, girl.

ROSAURA.   I swear I did not
Give him my picture, no, not yesterday.

ESTRELLA.   I'm satisfied. Forgive me my jealousy.

ROSAURA.   I understand it.

ESTRELLA.   Then you know it is
A monster that preys most where love is
     greatest.

ROSAURA.   I know.

ESTRELLA.   Then help me.

ROSAURA.   I will do your will.

ESTRELLA.   I am on fire. Astolfo treats me cruelly
But I love him the more. I burn for him,
I ache for him, Astraea. Yet I've sworn
That I will never speak to him again.
How may I then undo what I have said?

ROSAURA.   I think you cannot.

ESTRELLA.   No, I think I can.
Because our marriage is a thing of state
I've never spoken with the Duke in private.
I long to do so and to know his nature
To judge if he is fit to marry me.

ROSAURA.   Indeed?

ESTRELLA.   I have a bower in my garden
That's walled around, a pleasant secret place.
Give him this key and bid him enter in.
Say I'll be there tonight but do not tell him
I gave it to you but rather say you are
His friend, not mine. Take it, Astraea. Take it.

ROSAURA.   And when he comes, what then?

ESTRELLA.   I do not know.
Time must try that. Now I am wild with love

And I must have my will. I long for night
And for Astolfo. Heaven do me right.
(*Exit ESTRELLA.*)

ROSAURA.   I'll get a copy of this garden key:
Then when he comes, God knows who he
will see.

(*Exit ROSAURA. Enter KING BASILIO and ASTOLFO.*)

BASILIO.   But who can stop a bolting horse, Astolfo?
Or stop a river roaring to the sea?
Such is the pride and anger of the people:
Some shout "Astolfo," others "Sigismund."
My realm is turned into a stage for Fate
To play out monstrous tragedies of blood.

ASTOLFO.   I see I must forget my love awhile.
Now war must serve. This is no time for
wooing.
If Poland now resists me as her heir
It is because I have not proved myself,
And yet one day I'll sit upon her throne.
I'll take a horse. I'm proud and I am angry.
I'll strike those rebels like a thunderstone.
(*Exit ASTOLFO.*)

BASILIO.   O it is dangerous, foreseeing danger.
I ran away and ran to what I ran from.
I hid a thing, and hiding it I found it,
And so I have destroyed my own dear land.

(*Enter ESTRELLA.*)

ESTRELLA.   Your Majesty, you must go now in person
              And curb the turmoil raging in the streets,
              For everything is havoc and confusion.
              They clamour that you should release your
                 son.

(Enter CLOTALDO.)

CLOTALDO.   Thank God you're safe, sire.

BASILIO.   Where is Sigismund?

CLOTALDO.   The rebels found the tower and freed the Prince.

BASILIO.   Basil the Learned. What's my learning won?
              Basil the Great. What has my greatness done?
              This is the ruin of my lovely land.
              The winds have died. The stars, the sun have
                 gone.
              The houses and the farms stand now like
                 tombs.
              Each soldier is a walking skeleton.
              I see this nightmare with my eyes wide open;
              Before me stands an enormous hill
              Of men and horses, red and broken,
              And the whole hill cries out and will not be
                 still.

CLOTALDO.   There's some organ in man
              That seems to need death
              As the heart needs blood,
              As the lungs need breath.

ESTRELLA.   What I would do
Cannot now be done.
And yet there's a battle
Still to be won.

BASILIO.   Yes, I'll ride out
To meet my son.
(Exit KING BASILIO and ESTRELLA.)

CLOTALDO.   Why did he tell his son he was his father?
That has bred chaos. That was his mistake.
I'll never tell my daughter who I am
For fear lest Fortune throws me in the lake.

(Enter ROSAURA with her father's sword and a skull.)

ROSAURA.   The Duke must die.

CLOTALDO.   What would you now, Rosaura?
What is this show? What is this skull of death?

ROSAURA.   It is myself. For when Astolfo left me
I died. So he must die.

CLOTALDO.   No.

ROSAURA.   Hear me out.
Tonight he meets Estrella in a garden.
You told me that he woo'd in policy
But now I see it's lust. Then take this key
And this your sword and there cut down
    Astolfo.
Uphold my honour. Give me my revenge.

CLOTALDO.   Skulls, garden keys...Why this is fantasy.
             The Duke has gone to fight Prince Sigismund.

ROSAURA.   Then you must follow him.

CLOTALDO.   I cannot do that.

ROSAURA.   You swore to help me
             And you must keep your oath.

CLOTALDO.   I did plan for your honour's sake
             To kill him if I could,
             A tumble into the lake
             Or a garrotte in the wood.
             But then the young prince tried
             To crush me murderously
             And I surely would have died
             But Astolfo rescued me.
             I owe him my life, so how
             Can I kill him now?
             I'm bound to him and you:
             So what am I to do?

ROSAURA.   You are a man.
             You know the code.
             Giving is noble
             But receiving's base.
             You gave me life
             So I ennoble you.
             You received life from him
             So you owe him nothing.
             Do you accept that?

CLOTALDO.   Yes, in principle.
Yet though giving shows nobility
The generous must condemn
All those who react ungratefully
To those who succour them.
My reputation is unmarred
And I find meanness hateful.
My good name would be scarred
Were I to prove ungrateful.
I respect in my liberality
Giving and receiving equally.

ROSAURA.   You said to me that life
Without honour is no life,
So the life you gave me
Is no life at all.
And if being generous
Comes before being grateful
(As you seem to say),
I'm waiting for my life:
I haven't got it yet.

CLOTALDO.   You have convinced me.
But what can we do?
We must find you sanctuary.
I will give you all my wealth.
You shall live in a nunnery.
The advantages are three:
One, no civil feud;
Two, I deal generously;
Three, I show my gratitude.
There, I don't believe
I could hatch a better plot

If I was your father;
I'm sure I could not.

ROSAURA.   If you were my father
I'd take the insult:
Since you're not, I will not.
Money and a nunnery!

CLOTALDO.   Were I your father...

ROSAURA.   I would spit at you.

CLOTALDO.   You are forsworn
Because you swore to kill him.
Do not reproach me
If I am forsworn too.

ROSAURA.   Then I'll kill the Duke myself.

CLOTALDO.   I don't believe you.

ROSAURA.   I swear I will do it.

CLOTALDO.   You are a woman
And you have such courage?

ROSAURA.   Yes.

CLOTALDO.   What inspires you?

ROSAURA.   My good name.

CLOTALDO.   Astolfo
              Is going to be...

ROSAURA.   My honour.

CLOTALDO.   Both your King
              And your Estrella's husband.

ROSAURA.   I'll prevent him.
              By God, I swear it.

CLOTALDO.   This is madness.

ROSAURA.   Yes.

CLOTALDO.   Then stop it.

ROSAURA.   I cannot.

CLOTALDO.   Then you will lose...

ROSAURA.   I know I will.

CLOTALDO.   Your honour and your life.

ROSAURA.   I well believe it.

CLOTALDO.   What do you gain?

ROSAURA.   My death?

CLOTALDO.   This is mere spite.

ROSAURA.   It's honour.

CLOTALDO.   No, it's madness.

ROSAURA.   It's courage.

CLOTALDO.   No, it's frenzy.

ROSAURA.   No, it's rage:
                I call it rage.

CLOTALDO.   No, it is jealousy.
                You're jealous of your mistress.

ROSAURA.   I do not care if it's jealousy
                Or spite or rage or madness
                I have so many passions
                I don't know which is greatest.
                I will do it alone.
                (Exit ROSAURA.)

CLOTALDO.   Stars, show us all some shrewd way out of this,
                If you know one. O there is such confusion.
                Above the omens of the skies are bad.
                Below, it's worse. I fear the whole world's
                    mad.
                (Exit CLOTALDO.)

SCENE THREE

(Trumpets and drums. Enter SIGISMUND, armed, with his SOLDIERS.)

SIGISMUND.　I wish that Rome could see me here today,
　　　　　　Rome in her heyday, in her golden age.
　　　　　　Would not her legions laugh and whoop for joy
　　　　　　To see a wild beast marching at the head
　　　　　　Of such an army, great and proud enough
　　　　　　To conquer heaven? No, that's not the way
　　　　　　To mock illusion. Let's return to earth.
　　　　　　Before the gold sun sinks in the dark green sea
　　　　　　We will unthrone the King.

(Enter ASTOLFO, followed by ROSAURA on horseback.)

CLARION.　Here comes a horse, a tumultuous steed
　　　　　　(Pardon me, but I feel the need
　　　　　　To make a vivid, poetical speech)
　　　　　　Its mouth foams round the bit like a
　　　　　　sea-beach,
　　　　　　Its breath pounds like the hurricano,
　　　　　　Its heart pulses like a ripe volcano.
　　　　　　A horse of fire and water, earth and air:
　　　　　　Rosaura rides him. She is fair.

ROSAURA.　Honour: I wish to speak to you of honour.
　　　　　　Be generous, Sigismund. Your fame has sprung
　　　　　　From night's dim shadows into royal day,
　　　　　　And as the sun leaps from the arms of dawn
　　　　　　And bathes the hills and paints the shining
　　　　　　　sea-foam,

So may you now, that are the sun of Poland,
Shine upon me, a poor unhappy woman.
Three times we've met.
Three times you haven't known me.
First, I was a man
When you lay in prison
And your story eased me.
Second, I was a woman
When you were a King,
A dream King, a shadow.
Now I am whole,
I am both man and woman.
I had a love in Muscovy.
He is the Duke Astolfo.
He swore to marry me
But he broke his oath:
I seek revenge on him
As you seek it today
Against your royal father.

I wear both silk and steel.
Both of us wish to destroy this marriage.
I, that the man who is my lawful husband
May not be married to another woman;
You, to prevent Poland and Muscovy
Joining in one. Then as I am a woman,
Help me to win my honour. As I am man,
I say, go on and seize on Poland's crown;
Destroy Astolfo, do not let him have it.
Yet as I am woman, I beseech your pity
And pray you will be gentle now and kind.
Yet as I'm man, I offer you my sword.
But if you touch me as I am woman,

Then as I am a living breathing man,
I will defend my honour like a man
And I will kill you. In this war of love
I am a woman in my woe and fury,
But as I am a man, I'm strong for honour.

SIGISMUND.   What is the truth of this? I do not know.
If I have only dreamed my former greatness,
How can this woman speak of how she saw
    me?
Now counterfeits ring true and truth sounds
    hollow.
What does the shadow of a shadow look like?
What happens when two mirrors face each
    other?
If we cannot distinguish fact from fiction
Or what is real from what is an illusion,
Let's take the dream and use it to the limits
While we still can. Rosaura's in my power,
My heart shakes as her beauty shines on me.
What if she kneels? This is a dream. Enjoy it.
Regret it later. No, no. Work it out.
It is vainglory. All the good that's past
Is dreaming. We are born to disillusion.
Then if our pleasures are a little flame
Which the sharp wind will turn to ash and dust,
I'll hold to what is lasting and divine.
She tempts me but I'll turn from this
    temptation.
Sound the attack!
(*Alarum.*)

ROSAURA.   Sir, look at me.

> Look at me, my lord,
> Doesn't my honesty
> Deserve a single word?

SIGISMUND.   I look away because it's necessary.
Rosaura, if I am to save your honour
I must be cruel both to you and me.
I will not answer you but I will act.
Don't look at me, Rosaura, or my duty
Will be exterminated by your beauty.
I'll do you good if we thrive today
And save your honour. Soldiers, march away.
(Drums. Exit SIGISMUND and SOLDIERS.)

ROSAURA.   What do these riddles mean? He's clear and
strong
And will destroy a kingdom for revenge.
He is awake,
But I am...I am I.
(Sings.)
Dreamed the world was simple
Sweet and gentle-eyed.
But when I woke up
There was a monster at my side.
Dreamed that I had thought of
A cunning clever scheme.
Then I began to laugh,
Like a clown in a dream.

(Alarums. Enter CLARION.)

CLARION.   With banners flowing and trumpets thrilling
The King is going to do some killing.

ROSAURA.   I'll throw myself with joy into this chaos.
            I'll ride and fight beside Prince Sigismund,
            The scandal and the wonder of the world.
            (Exit ROSAURA. Alarums.)

CLARION.   Battle rages, let the hero
            Hack his way into the middle.
            I will play the role of Nero
            At a distance on the fiddle.
            If I want to feel compassion
            I'll feel sorry for myself.
            Watch the guns and sabres flashing,
            Unmolested on my shelf.
            (Climbs up. Music continues.)
            From up here I'll watch the show,
            Safely from this perch of mine.
            Death won't find me up here, so
            I can give him the old sign.
            (CLARION hides above.)

        (Alarums. Enter ASTOLFO.)

ASTOLFO.   A sword has cut my vein:
            I bleed to death.
            Is there nobody by
            To bind my wound?
            Is no one here among
            These cruel rocks?
            I faint. Help. Help me now.

        (Enter ROSAURA on horseback.)

ROSAURA.   My name is Death.

ASTOLFO.   Lo, here's another furore.

ROSAURA.   I am your death.

ASTOLFO.   Those are words, Rosaura.
I know you well from when we both were
    wooing:
You're good at talking but less good at doing.
You love to act but this is not a stage.
This blood is real. So is your father's sword.
Then keep your oath, Rosaura, if you can.
(She unhorses and binds his wounds.)
I like you best when silent.

*(Alarums. Enter BASILIO, ESTRELLA and CLOTALDO in
retreat.)*

BASILIO.   I need a new name. Basilio the broken-hearted.

ESTRELLA.   The traitors triumph.

CLOTALDO.   Your army has deserted.

BASILIO.   All meanings change when a battle's done.
Traitors are patriots if they've won.

ESTRELLA.   Now we must hide from your tyrannous son.

*(Shot within. CLARION falls wounded from his hiding-
place.)*

CLARION.   Heaven and Hell! I think I'm done.

ASTOLFO.   Who is this fellow?

CLOTALDO.   Somebody's son.

CLARION.   Got any brandy? Hurts where I fell down.

ASTOLFO.   Who are you, man?

CLARION.   I'm just a bloody clown.
Hey! Can I give you
One bit of advice?
If you want to survive,
You ought to pick
The part where the battle
Is really thick,
Where the corpses pile up
In a rough pyramid.
It's a damn sight safer
Than hiding like I did.
You can't escape Fate,
The stars do not lie.
When God wants it
We have to die.
Hey friend, pass the cup.
(CLOTALDO gives him a drink.)
Strange, it feels
Like I'm waking up.
(Sings.)
A clown in a dream
Falling upside down
And when I woke up
I was a dream in a clown.
(Dies.)

BASILIO.   When God wants it we have to die:
That truth is written in the sky.

CLOTALDO.   Yet it's not Christianity to state
There's no defence against men's fate.
(Takes up CLARION's jacket and cap.)
Disguise yourself, and hide and wait.

ESTRELLA.   A horse is over here: he is swift and fleet.

ASTOLFO.   Ride off. We'll cover your retreat.

BASILIO.   No, I'll await death in this place:
I want to look him in the face.
*(Alarum. CLOTALDO disguises BASILIO in
CLARION's clothes.)*

ASTOLFO.   Take it and fly.

CLOTALDO.   And we will guard the way.

ESTRELLA.   Make haste, my lord.

ASTOLFO.   Escape while you still may.

(Alarum. Enter SOLDIERS. They find BASILIO's robe.)

1ST SOLDIER. The King's in hiding here.

2ND SOLDIER. Seek him out. And Astolfo.

1ST SOLDIER. Search every cave and rock.

CLOTALDO.   O fly, my lord.

BASILIO.   Clotaldo, stand aside.

(Enter SIGISMUND, horsed. BASILIO steps forward.)

> Your hunt is over,
> Prince, I am here.
> Now make your carpet
> Of my grizzled hair.
> I am your prisoner.
> Do what you must do:
> Let the predictions
> Of the stars come true.

SIGISMUND *(to audience)*.

> You who have witnessed these high words
>   and deeds,
> Listen to me. Attend your lawful Prince.
> *(He dismounts.)*
> Those star words, written by God
> On the blue tablet of the sky,
> Those books with diamond letters
> Printed on sapphire pages,
> They never cheat or lie.
> The one who lies and cheats
> Is the man who claims
> He understands the stars.
> My father to protect himself
> Made me a beast-man.
> I could have been gentle,
> But raised in a monster's den

Of course I grew up
A monstrosity.

If it was prophesied that you would be
Killed by a beast, would it be sensible
For you to seek out sleeping beasts or
    beast-men
And wake them up? If you were warned,
    "the sword
You wear will be your death," would it be
    sense
To carry that same sword between your teeth?
If someone said, "A green and silver mass
Of salty water will be your sad grave,"
Would it be sense to sail forth on the sea-waves
When they hurl up their curling, snow-topped
    peaks?
With all your wisdom this is what you did.

Look at this man. He tried to rule the stars
Yet now he kneels before me and is humble.
How can I quell the hate he's bred in me?
What shall I do? What is my way? My answer?
What's right for me to do at this brief moment?
My soul cries out for vengeance but I see
My victory must be my own surrender.
Sir, now that heaven has proved you wrong,
    I kneel
And offer you my neck to tread upon.

BASILIO.   My son, my own son,
                    By this act I am reborn inside you.
                    You have overcome yourself.

You have overcome the stars.
You have won yourself a crown.
(*BASILIO crowns and robes SIGISMUND.*
Drums and trumpets.)

ALL.   King Sigismund.

SIGISMUND.   Then all of you mark well
How I mean to rule in Poland.
Since I would be a conqueror
I see that I must first
Make a conquest of myself.
Astolfo, you have a debt
To pay from long ago.
Take Rosaura by the hand
And pay the debt you owe.

ASTOLFO.   It's true there's a debt and obligation,
But think: she does not even know her name.
It would be base to wed...

CLOTALDO.   No, say no more.
Rosaura is as noble as yourself:
She is my daughter.
You loved me well, girl, when you were my
     niece;
Then will you hate me now I am your father?

ROSAURA.   I cannot tell.

ASTOLFO.   What, is this true?

CLOTALDO.   I did not wish it known

Until I saw her honourably married.
She is my daughter.

ASTOLFO.   Then since this is so,
And I have no hope to rule in Poland
I'll keep my word. Give my your hand,
    Rosaura,
We're both forsworn.

SIGISMUND *(to ROSAURA)*.   Come, take what you
          have dreamed of.
Clotaldo, you were loyal both to me
And to my father. Ask me anything
And I will grant it you.

CLOTALDO.   Then ask my daughter
To forgive me.

SIGISMUND.   So I do. Embrace your father.
Now for Estrella. She must not be left
Unhappy by the loss of such a prince.
Lady, I'll find you out another husband
Who is, I think, as good in birth and fortune.
Give me your hand. You shall be Poland's
          Queen.

ESTRELLA.   I am content. It is good policy,
And so I trust I may in time be happy.

1ST SOLDIER. What about us? Clotaldo fought against you
          And yet you honour him. We made you King,

Rescued you from the tower and fought beside
   you:
What's our reward?

SIGISMUND.   The tower. Chains. No daylight.
There is no need of traitors
When the work of treason's done.

ASTOLFO.   How changed he is.

ROSAURA.   How wise.

BASILIO.   How like a king.

SIGISMUND.   Do I surprise you? Do not be amazed.
Is it a wonder if a dream has taught me
A little wisdom, I should fear to wake
And find myself once more a prisoner?
(To audience.)
Yet even if that time never arrives,
I believe now that all human lives
Are just like dreams. They come, they go.
Perfection is impossible, we know.
Then noble hearts, show mercy, thus,
And for our worst faults, gently pardon us.
Remember as you each pass on your way,
Our actors, our musicians and our play.

THE END